My Best EVER BIBLE!

Noah's Ark

N oah! Noah! Listen to me!" It was God speaking. Noah looked up from his work.

"Yes, God," he said, putting down his tools. "What is it?"

"I want you to build a big wooden boat—an ark," God said. "It's got to be big enough for all your family and two of every kind of animal."

"But why?" Noah asked. He was puzzled, for the sea was far away.

"All over the beautiful world that I made, people are fighting each other," God replied. "So, I'm going to send a flood to destroy everything. But you will be safe in the ark."

God wanted to save Noah, because he was the only good man left on the whole earth.

"Come on, everyone! We've got work to do!" cried Noah to his family, and they set about building the ark just as God wanted—with three decks, a roof, rooms inside, a door, and tar on the outside to make it waterproof.

Phew!

4

Other people thought they were crazy, but Noah just smiled and continued working. They measured and sawed, and hammered and sanded, until finally the ark was finished.

We're in the desert, you nincompoop!

Next, Noah called to all the animals to come in twos.
It was tricky getting them all on board safely,
without anyone being squashed.
But at last the great big door was shut tight.

The sky grew black. The wind howled. And it began to rain. And rain.

Soon there was water all around. The ark started to float.

And the water rose higher...

and higher...

until it covered the top of the highest mountain.

Then, suddenly, the rain stopped. And the water started going down.

BUMP!

Before long, Noah realized they weren't moving anymore—they were stuck!

Noah sent out a raven. But it did not return. So, he sent out a dove. It came back, carrying a twig. They all cheered...

Hooray!

and scanned the horizon, looking for dry land.

Then, a few weeks later, there was a cry from the lookout.

Land ho!

When the water had finally gone, Noah opened
the door of the ark, and everyone hurried out.
It was wonderful to feel the earth beneath their feet.

Curved across the sky was a beautiful rainbow. And God said, "I promise that I will never send another flood over the world. And, Noah, you will never have to build another ark again!"

Thank goodness for that!

Samson, the Strongest Man in the World

Once there was a boy named Samson.

Before he was born, an angel appeared to his mother and said, "Soon you will have a baby boy—even though you thought you'd never have children. This baby will be special to God, and you must never cut his hair."

So, as Samson grew up, his parents never cut his hair. It grew longer and longer.

"Soon it'll reach his knees!" whispered his friends.

I'm special!

But Samson didn't mind what anyone said. He had a secret.

He was strong—stronger than an ox, stronger even than a lion. He was stronger than anyone else in the world. And that was because he did as God said and never cut his hair.

Once, he fought against thirty men—and beat them easily.

Another time, he fought a thousand!

SPLAT!

OOF!

Samson's enemies, the Philistines, wanted to stop him. They thought he was too powerful.

Now, Samson loved a girl named Delilah. So the Philistines said to Delilah, "Find out what makes Samson so strong. Then we'll give you lots of money."

Delilah asked Samson. He replied, "If you tie me up with seven bowstrings, I'll be as weak as a mouse."

But it was a trick!

"Tie me up with new ropes," he said next. "I won't be strong then." But that was a trick, too. The ropes pinged off him as if they were thin cotton thread.

"Tie me up by my hair," he said then. But guess what...?

Ha ha!
Tricked you again!

Finally, he told Delilah, "The reason I'm so strong is because my hair has never been cut. If anyone cut it, I'd be just as weak as the next man." Delilah realized this was the real secret and hurried off to tell the Philistines.

While Samson was asleep, the Philistines came and cut all his hair.

They put him in chains and led him away to prison.
Samson tried to fight back, but it was no use.

But slowly, slowly, Samson's hair began to grow. And
as it grew back, something else happened. Samson
began to get stronger and stronger.

One day, some Philistine kings and many thousands of their followers gathered in a temple for a celebration. They called for Samson, so that they could make fun of him.

Samson was desperate to get back at the Philistines. So he prayed to God, "Make me really strong—just once more!"

He put his hands against the temple pillars beside him, and he pushed with all his might. They creaked and they groaned, and then...

...the whole building fell down, killing everyone inside. And that was the end of Samson's enemies—but it was also the end of the strongest man in the world.

David and Goliath

The Israelites in King Saul's army were getting ready for war. They could see their enemy, the Philistines, on the other side of the valley.

Suddenly, everyone stopped and stared.

Someone from the enemy was walking toward them.

Someone

huge.

35

The giant strode along; his bronze armor gleamed and winked in the sun, blinding whoever looked at him.

His voice boomed out: "Israelites! Listen to me!
I am Goliath, a Philistine. I dare one of you to fight me!
If I lose, we Philistines will become your slaves.

"But if I win, you will be *our* slaves."

The Israelites were terrified.

King Saul saw how scared they were. "I'll give a big reward to whoever fights this Goliath," he said.

But no one wanted to do it. All of them were too frightened. All except a young shepherd boy named David, who was visiting his brothers.

"I'll fight him," said David bravely. "I'll be all right—God's on our side."

But King Saul shook his head. "You mustn't," he said. "You're just a boy."

"Your Majesty," replied David, "when I guard my father's sheep, I have to fight lions and bears. With God's help I can kill anything, even this big bully."

"Very well," agreed King Saul. "Here's my armor and my sword."

David put it on, but immediately fell over! "I can't wear this heavy stuff!" he cried, and took it all off again.

Instead, he took his shepherd's sling and picked out five smooth pebbles from the stream. Now, he was ready.

Goliath began walking toward David. As he got nearer, he burst out laughing.

"Are you going to fight me? You must be joking!"

But David answered, "I'm fighting in the name of God—and I'm going to win! You'll see!"

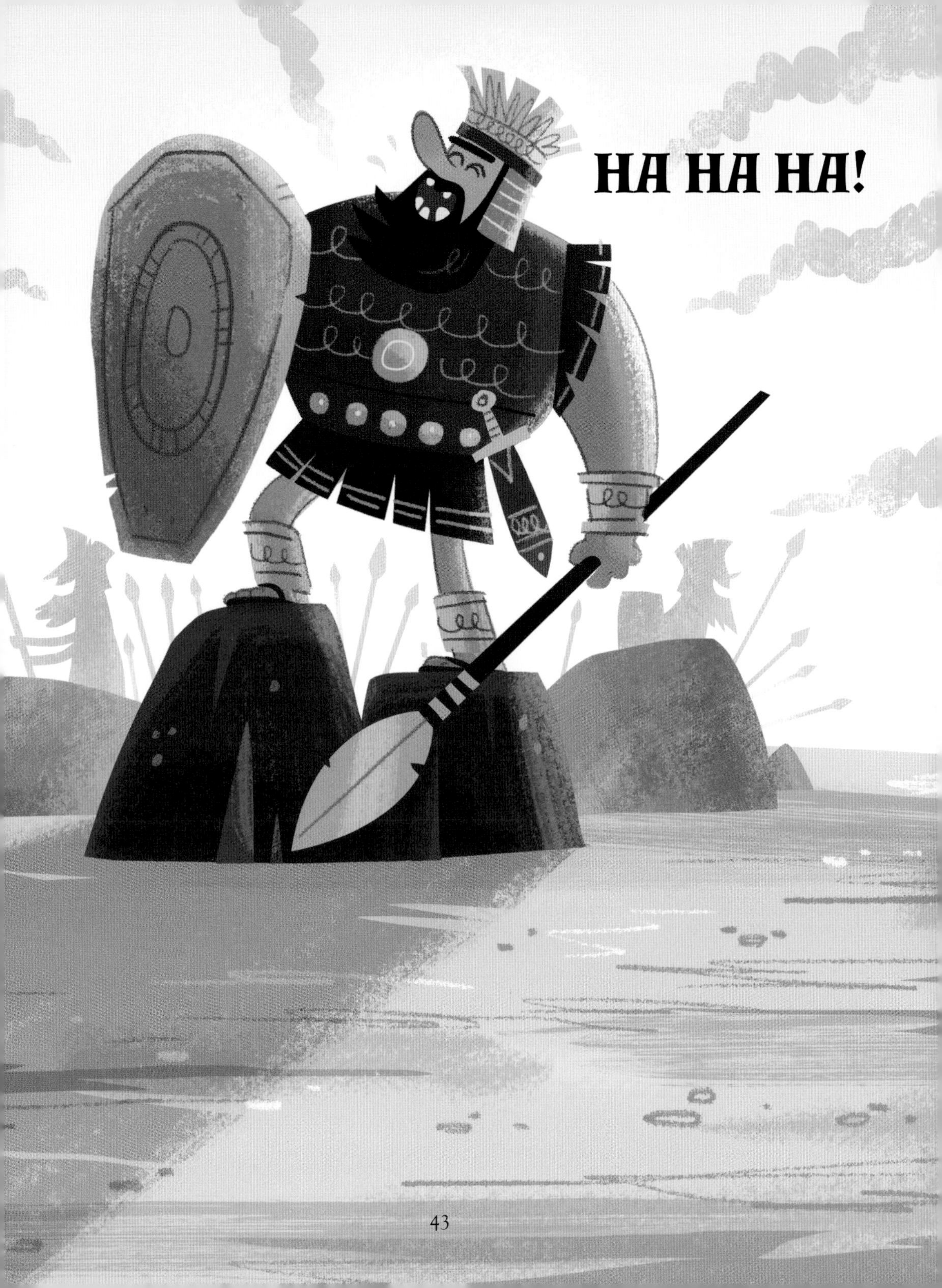
HA HA HA!

David put a pebble into his sling and flung it as hard as he could at Goliath. It hit him square on the forehead, and the giant fell crashing to the ground.

When the Philistines saw that Goliath was dead, they turned and fled. Shouting loudly, the Israelites chased after them, right into the next valley and beyond.

Go away!

And the young shepherd boy David became the new hero of Israel!

Well done!

Hooray!

48

Daniel and the Lions

King Darius was the king of Babylon. But Daniel was the one who was really in charge. He was nearly as important as the king himself.

The king's other helpers didn't like Daniel.
"He's such a goody-goody," said the first helper.
"Let's trick him into doing something wrong,"
said the second helper.

The only problem was that Daniel never did
anything wrong.
"I've got an idea," said the third helper. "Listen..."

The next day the helpers went to the king.

"Your Majesty, we think you should make a new law," said the first helper. "No one is allowed to ask for anything, unless it's from you. If they do, they must be thrown into a den . . .

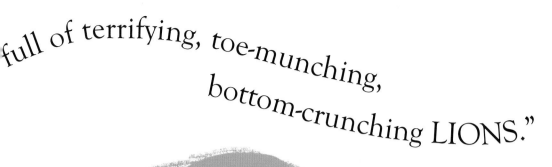

full of terrifying, toe-munching, bottom-crunching LIONS."

"Basically, he'll be gobbled up," added the second helper.

"Until he's dead," said the third helper.

"Yes, I get it. Um, okay," agreed King Darius.

When Daniel went home, he knelt down at his window and prayed to God, as he always did.

Please, God, help me to be good.

The three helpers rushed to the palace. "Your Majesty, Daniel's broken your new law!" they cried.

King Darius was very upset. He liked Daniel a lot. But the law was the law.

"I hope your God can save you," he said sadly, as Daniel was led away by the guards.

The lions padded around the den. Their sharp teeth glinted. And their great manes shook as they snarled.

RRAAHH!

The helpers looked on gleefully. "Watch your toes, Daniel! And your–"

But then the guards placed a large stone over the entrance.

That evening the king was angry and fidgety. And when he finally went to bed, he could not sleep a wink. All he could think about was poor Daniel. What were the lions doing to him?

The next morning the king rushed to the den.

"Daniel!"
he shouted.

"Are you all right?"

To his amazement,
Daniel shouted in reply,

"I'm fine!
God stopped
the lions from
hurting me."

Back at the palace King Darius said to Daniel, "Now, I will make a new law: everyone must pray to your God." Daniel was happy—everything had come out all right.

But not for the helpers.

"Take them away!" King Darius said to the guards. "You know where!"

And, that day, the lions didn't go hungry.

Nice toes!

Jonah and the Whale

Once there was a man named Jonah.

One day God said, "Jonah! Go to Nineveh and tell the people there to stop doing bad things. Tell them that if they don't, I'll punish them!"

NINEVEH

JOPPA

THE SEA

But Jonah didn't want to go to Nineveh. *I know,* he thought. *I'll run away to sea. God won't find me there.*

At the port of Joppa, Jonah found a ship. "One ticket to Spain, please," he said to the captain.

As soon as they set off, a great storm blew up. Waves as high as a house crashed over the deck, and the wind ripped through the sails.

"There must be a reason for this!" said the captain. "Someone's to blame."

Jonah sighed and told the captain and his crew about running away from God. At that moment, the mast creaked and the ship tipped.

Aaah! We're going to die!

"Throw me into the sea," said Jonah sadly. "Then the storm will stop."

So that's what they did.

The wind dropped and the waves grew still. And Jonah sank

down

down

down

down

into the stomach of an enormous fish.

It was dark and lonely in there. Jonah had time to think. And to pray.

"O, God, thank you for saving me. From now on I will always praise you!"

After three days, the fish spat Jonah out onto a beach. He was slimy and hungry, but very glad to be alive.

God spoke to him again: "Now, go to the people of Nineveh and give them my message."
So Jonah did.

Much to his surprise, they were very sorry for being bad. And God said he wouldn't punish them after all.

Jonah was angry. "Why have you let them off? That's so unfair!"

God replied, "You have no reason to be angry, Jonah."

Jonah said nothing, but left the city and made a shelter. In the night a plant grew, which gave him more shade the next day.

But it withered in the sun.
Jonah was furious!

Humph!

"Why are you sorry that this plant died?" said God.
"You didn't make it grow. But if you can be sorry for a
plant, perhaps you'll understand why I can be sorry for
the people of Nineveh."

And, finally, Jonah understood how much God loves people and how he is always ready to forgive, no matter what they have done.

The Baby Jesus

One evening, a man and a woman on a donkey arrived at a little town called Bethlehem.

"Thank goodness we're here, Joseph," said Mary. "I'm sure my baby will come soon."

Now, they just needed somewhere to stay.

But there was no room anywhere! Finally, Joseph tried a small, shabby-looking place on the edge of town.

The innkeeper came to the door. "I'm sorry, there's no space here," he said. "But you're welcome to stay in the stable at the back."

The little stable was warm and snug. Joseph made a bed for Mary, and soon her baby was born. Mary wrapped him up and laid him in the manger.

Out on the hillsides, shepherds were guarding their sheep.

"Look at that star," said one. "It's much bigger than the others."

At that moment a dazzling brightness lit up the sky. It was an angel!

"Be happy, everyone!" said the angel. "God's Son has been born in Bethlehem. Go, and see him. You'll find him lying in a manger."

Suddenly, the sky was filled with angels singing and praising God. Once they had left, the shepherds were stunned.

And immediately they set off for Bethlehem.

Far away in the East, three wise men were looking up at the sky.

"That bright star is telling us that a king has been born," said one. "We must find him. The star will show us the way."

In Jerusalem they went to the palace. "We're looking for a baby king—the king of the Jews," they said.

"We've been following his star and we want to worship him."

King Herod was angry. He was the only king! He summoned some priests and teachers. "Where will this king be born?" he demanded.

"The holy books say he will be born in the town of Bethlehem, Your Majesty," they told him.

Herod thought for a moment and then turned to the wise men with a toothy smile. "The baby is in Bethlehem," he said. "When you have found him, do tell me where he is so that I may also worship him." Herod had a secret plan—to kill the baby!

The wise men journeyed on until they reached
Bethlehem.

They gave Jesus the special presents they had brought:

gold

frankincense

myrrh

God sent an angel in a dream to warn the wise men
not to go back to Herod. So, they returned to the East
another way.

Joseph, Mary, and Jesus also escaped—to Egypt, far from wicked King Herod.

And, when it was safe to come back, they went to Nazareth, in Galilee, where they made their home.

The Good Samaritan

When Jesus grew up, he spent much of his time talking to people about God. One day, a teacher of the religious laws said to him, "What must I do to be with God in heaven forever?"

Jesus asked him, "What does it say in the Scriptures?"

The man replied, "'Love God and love my neighbor.' But who is my neighbor?"
So Jesus told him a story.

"One day, a man was walking from Jerusalem to Jericho.

"Suddenly he felt a THWACK! on his back and a THUMP! on his head.

THWACK!   **THUMP!**

"When he opened his eyes, he was sitting in the road. Where was his stick? Gone. His money? Gone. His clothes? Nearly all gone.

"And the robbers? Definitely gone.

"It hurt too much to move, so the man just lay down and waited for someone to help him.

"After a little while, he heard something. *At last!* thought the man.

  "A priest was on his way to Jerusalem. With a great effort, the man lifted his head and moaned.

Help!

Ugh!

"The priest glanced at him, wrinkled his nose in disgust, and crossed to the other side of the road. He certainly didn't want to be bothered with someone half naked and covered in bruises.

"Sometime later, the man heard more footsteps. It was a Levite, a worker from the Temple. But he, too, crossed to the other side of the road and hurried along, trying to forget what he had seen.

"Now, the man in the road was sure he would die—for nobody would help him.

Help!

I'm far too busy.

"But what was this? Some kind words, a gentle touch... The man opened one eye and saw a Samaritan next to him."

Here—drink this.

The teacher listening to the story raised his eyebrows in surprise, as Samaritans and Jews didn't usually go near each other.

Jesus continued, "The Samaritan bandaged up the injured man's wounds, lifted him onto his donkey, and took him to an inn.

"For the rest of the day, the Samaritan looked after him.

"The next morning, he said to the innkeeper, 'Here's some money. Please, take care of this man, and when I come back I will pay you more if necessary.'

"'Yes, sir,' replied the innkeeper, and before long the wounded man was better."

Jesus asked the teacher of the religious laws, "Who acted like a neighbor to the man who was robbed?"

The teacher said, "The man who was kind to him."

Jesus said, "If you want to be a good neighbor, you must go and do the same."

The teacher sighed. Now he understood—he had to be kind to everyone he met!

The Prodigal Son

One day a group of tax collectors and religious teachers gathered around Jesus.

"Why do you spend time with bad people?" they asked him. "You talk to them and even have dinner with them. It doesn't make sense!"

So Jesus told them a story.

"There was once a man who had two sons.

"One day, the younger son said, 'Father, I know I will get my share of your land when you die. But please, can I have it now?'

"'Very well,' agreed his father.

"And immediately the younger son sold the land and left home with a bag full of gold coins.

It's party time!

"He journeyed to a country far away and began a new life there. But he kept spending money...

and soon there was none left.

"That year there was a terrible famine. Everyone was hungry—and the younger son grew thinner and thinner, and hungrier and hungrier.

"He got a job looking after some pigs. But no one gave *him* any food.

Even the pigs eat more than I do!

"So, he decided to go back to his father's house and work as a servant.

"On the way, he became more and more worried about seeing his father. Why had he spent all that money?

"Outside the house his father was looking at the figure in the distance coming along the road. Could it be...? Surely not...

"Yes, it was!

"He ran to his son and hugged him again and again. 'My son! You're back!' And he wept tears of joy.

"'Father, I have done wrong,' said the younger son. 'I'm so sorry.'

"But his father waved to the servants. 'Hurry!' he shouted. 'Give him fine clothes and kill our best calf. We'll have a feast!'

"The older son came in from working in the fields. He was very angry.

"'It's so unfair!' he yelled. 'For years I have worked for you, day in, day out. And what do I get? Nothing! Yet he wastes all his money and you throw him a party!'

"The father replied gently, 'My son, everything I have is yours. But we must celebrate, for your brother was dead and is now alive. He was lost, but is found!'"

Jesus said to the crowd, "In the same way, God's love is for all people, including those who are bad. And when they are sorry, God is just as happy as the father whose son came back to him."

Jesus and
the Tax Collector

One morning, Jesus was passing through the town of Jericho with his friends. They were on their way to Jerusalem.

By this time, Jesus was well known for his teaching and for healing those who were sick, and so lots of people wanted to see him and talk to him.

Look—here he comes!

Please help me!

One man who couldn't see a thing was Zacchaeus, the tax collector.

"It's so unfair being small," he grumbled for the thousandth time, pushing his way through the crowd.

Oy, you!

**Stop it,
Zacchaeus!**

"All my life I've had
this problem!"

Then, Zacchaeus had an idea. "If I run ahead," he said thoughtfully, "I could climb the big tree near the road. Then I'd definitely get a good view of Jesus!"

Squawk!

So, huffing and puffing, he jogged to the tree and pulled himself up the trunk and onto a sturdy branch. "Ha! Made it!"

Zacchaeus was very happy. All he had to do now was wait for Jesus to come along.

From time to time someone pointed at him and laughed.

Ha ha ha!

No one in Jericho liked Zacchaeus. Collecting taxes will never get you many friends—and Zacchaeus was always making people pay more than they needed to and keeping any extra money for himself.

After a while the people moved closer, and Zacchaeus leaned forward. To his great surprise they stopped right by his tree.

"Zacchaeus, climb down!" called Jesus. "I'm coming to stay with you."

"What?!" everyone exclaimed. But Zacchaeus slid down to the ground as fast as he could.

Beaming with pride, Zacchaeus led Jesus away, while the crowd muttered and mumbled.

It's not right!

But he's a cheat!

I'm MUCH more important than Zacchaeus!

141

Inside Zacchaeus's house, Jesus and the tax collector spent a long time talking. And the longer they talked, the sadder Zacchaeus looked. "I'm sorry," he said finally, in a very small voice.

A short time later, Zacchaeus came out with Jesus by
his side.

"I have something to tell you all!" he said loudly to
the crowd. "I'm going to give half my money to the
poor. And if I've cheated anyone, I'll pay them four
times as much as I owe them."

Jesus said, "You have done the right thing, Zacchaeus. Now, you can start a new life being good. And it will make you much happier."

Hooray!

Well done!

The Easter Story

Clink
Clink

"Just look at these beauties! Thirty silver coins!" cackled
Judas.

Judas was Jesus's friend. But he was greedy and had
made a secret deal with some priests. They would give
him a bag of silver, and he would show them where
Jesus was. He knew the priests wanted to arrest Jesus.

And now the moment had come. "I'll give Jesus a kiss," he whispered to the priests' guards. "That's how you'll know it's him."

Judas and the guards came to an olive grove. There was Jesus, praying. And his friends, sleeping.

Judas went up to Jesus and kissed him on the cheek. The guards immediately surrounded Jesus and held his arms tightly.

"Let go of him!" shouted Peter, jumping up. But they took Jesus away.

Then all Jesus's friends ran off, afraid that they, too, would be arrested.

The priests asked Jesus questions all night. But no one could prove he'd done anything wrong—only that he let others say he was the Son of God.

The next morning was Friday. Jesus was brought before the Roman governor, Pontius Pilate.

"Why did you bring him to me?" asked Pilate. "He hasn't committed a crime."

But then Pilate saw the crowds. He knew there could be trouble.

At this time of year a prisoner was usually set free. "Shall I let this man go or Barabbas?" Pilate shouted.

Barabbas!

Barabbas!

Barabbas was a murderer.
"Barabbas! Barabbas!" they chanted.
"So, what should I do with Jesus?" Pilate asked.
"Kill him!" they yelled.

Kill him!

Pilate shrugged his shoulders
and handed Jesus over.

The guards placed a crown of thorns on Jesus's head. They spat on him and hit him.

Then they took him to a place named Golgotha, which means "the place of the skull."

Jesus was put on a cross in between two criminals. At about three o'clock he gave a loud cry—and died.

The earth shook and rocks split apart. Everyone was scared and stood still, watching. When all was quiet again, Jesus's friends walked sadly away.

He was definitely the Son of God!

Later that day, a man named Joseph from Arimathea placed Jesus's body in a tomb and rolled a large stone across the entrance.

On Sunday morning, Mary Magdalene set off to look at Jesus's body. When she arrived, she stopped and stared. The stone had been rolled back, and the tomb was empty!

Mary ran back to fetch Peter and John, and she showed them the empty tomb. Neither of them could understand what had happened, and so they left, puzzled and sad.

Mary felt very alone.

"Why are you crying?" came a man's voice.

"I just want to know where they have taken him," she wept.

The man said, "Mary!"

And then she knew—it was Jesus. He was alive again!

And all was well.

Good Books books may be purchased in bulk at special discounts for sales promotion, corporate gifts, fund-raising, or educational purposes. Special editions can also be created to specifications. For details, contact the Special Sales Department, Good Books, 307 West 36th Street, 11th Floor, New York, NY 10018 or info@skyhorsepublishing.com.

Good Books is an imprint of Skyhorse Publishing, Inc.®, a Delaware corporation.

Visit our website at www.goodbooks.com.

10 9 8 7 6 5 4 3 2 1

Library of Congress Cataloging-in-Publication Data is available on file.

Cover design and illustration by Lion Hudson plc

Print ISBN: 978-1-68099-186-4

Printed in China